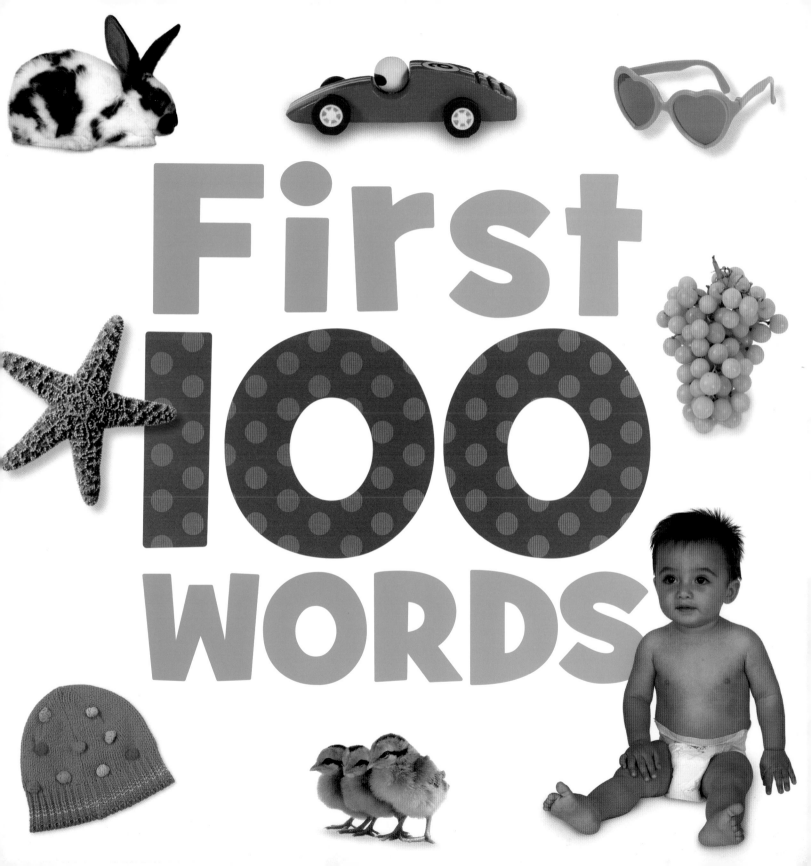

First 100 WORDS

Family

mommy

brother

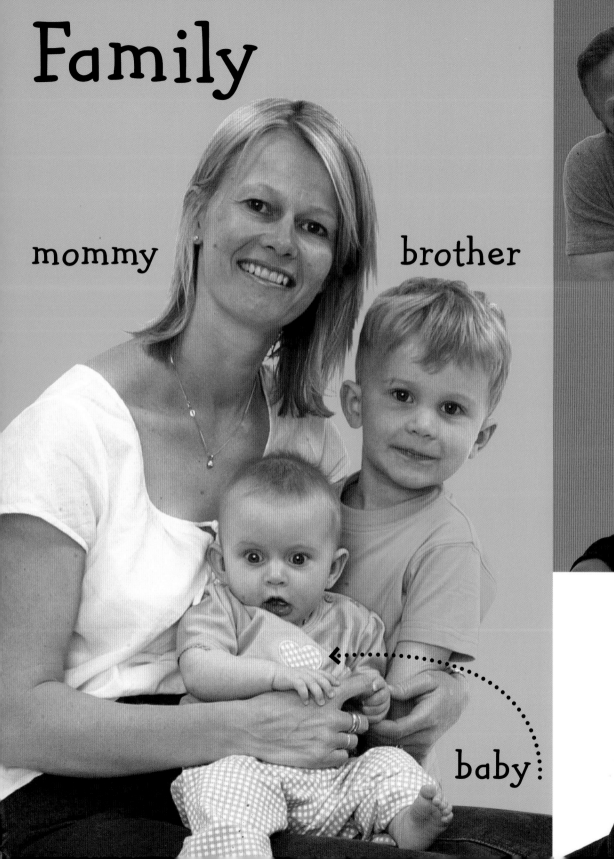

baby

daddy

aunt

uncle

grandpa

sister
girl

boy

grandma

cousin

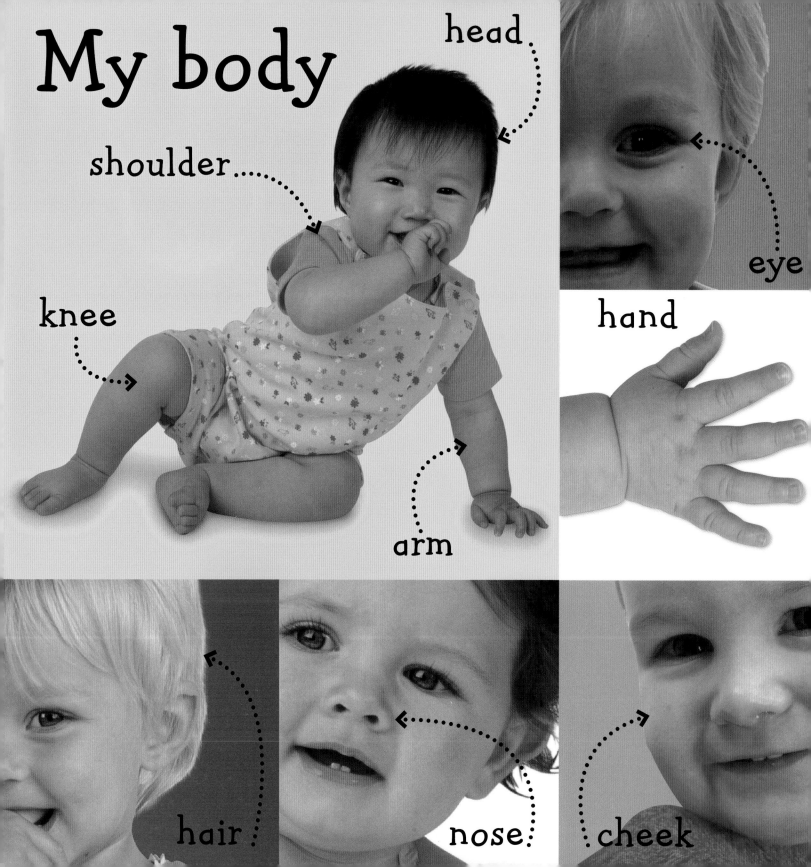

My body

head

shoulder

knee

arm

eye

hand

hair

nose

cheek

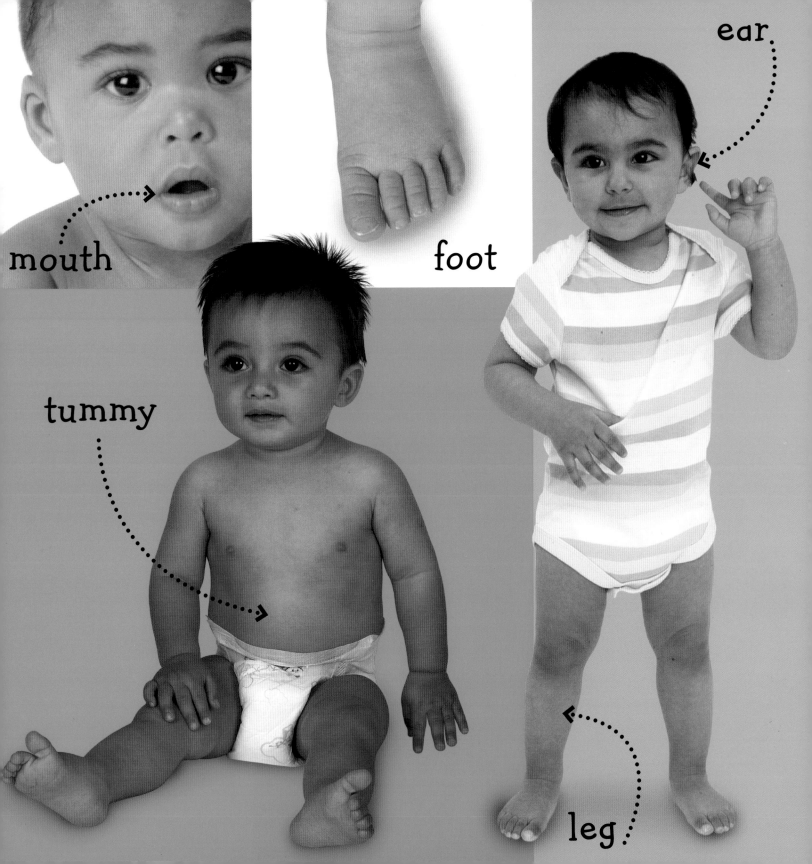

mouth

foot

ear

tummy

leg

Getting dressed

shorts

hat

skirt

sweater

T-shirt

jeans

pants

jacket

sock

dress

slippers

scarf

mittens

shoes

Food

cucumber

pear

apple

cookie

carrots

grapes

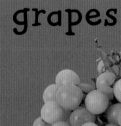

oranges

broccoli

strawberries

bread

yogurt

cheese

tomato

banana

Toys and games

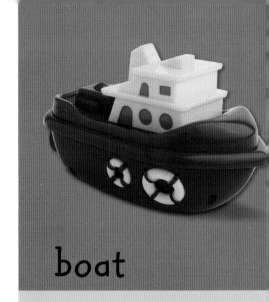

boat

car

book.

ball

train

teddy bear

building blocks

doll

Pets

dog

parrot

kitten

guinea pig

cat

rabbit

goldfish

puppy

hamster

On the farm

hen

duck

cow

duckling

piglet

pig

goat

sheep

chicks

lamb

horse

foal

geese

At the zoo

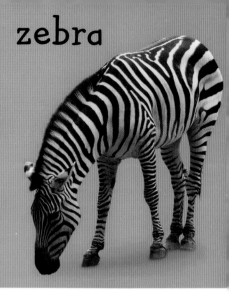

zebra

bear

monkey

tiger

elephant

lion

rhinoceros

snake

giraffe

At the beach

starfish

sand
castle

swimsuit

crab

sunglasses

rubber tube

shell

swimming trunks

straw hat

pinwheel

bucket

shovel

Bath time

towel

bath

bubbles

toy duck

soap

toothbrush

sponge

Bedtime

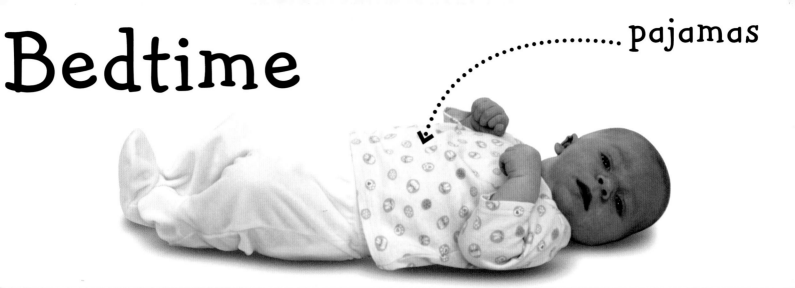

pajamas

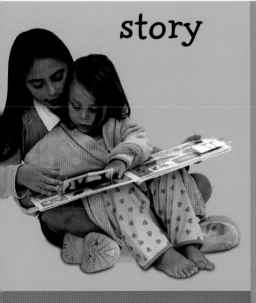

story

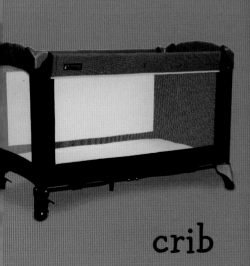

crib

blanket

Colors

white

black

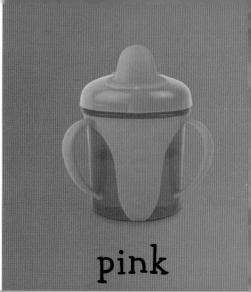

pink

yellow

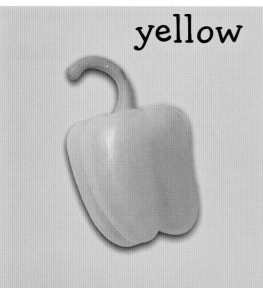

green

blue

red

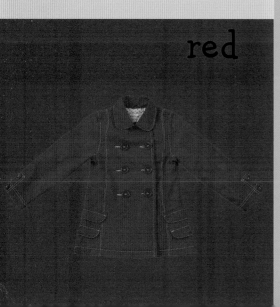

Shapes

rectangle

circle

square

star

heart

triangle

Numbers

1
baby

2 chicks

3 cupcakes

4 puppies

5 flowers